Original title:
The Great Search for Life's Missing Puzzle Piece

Copyright © 2025 Creative Arts Management OÜ
All rights reserved.

Author: Elias Montgomery
ISBN HARDBACK: 978-1-80566-064-4
ISBN PAPERBACK: 978-1-80566-359-1

The Quest for Unity Amidst Discord

In a world of mismatched socks,
We hunt for comfort, not for rocks.
We've lost the map, it's upside down,
Searching for joy in every town.

With coffee cups that spill and slide,
We've tripped on dreams, but laughed with pride.
The puzzle pieces aren't in sight,
Yet giggles bloom in the moonlight.

In gardens where the daisies spun,
We chased the sun, had way more fun.
The missing piece was maybe cake,
Or laughter that we dare to make.

So here's the key, let's dance along,
In silly hats, we sing our song.
Though chaos swirls like a wild breeze,
Together, friends, we find our ease.

Unearthing the Missing Nexus

In the attic, I found a sock,
A relic of my missing clock.
Thought I'd find the answers there,
Instead, I met a dusty bear.

Googled my obsessions tight,
Maybe my dog is wrong or right.
Life's puzzle missing one big piece,
Could it be in my sandwich's crease?

Discerning Patterns in the Chaos

I counted clouds, I wrote a song,
But the notes keep running wrong.
Am I lost in this berry maze?
Or just stuck in a jammed craze?

The cat stares at me, unimpressed,
While I ponder who's the best.
Was it popcorn or was it fries?
My brain might just need to reprise.

In Search of the Resonant Note

I strummed a chord on my new lute,
But the sound was more like a hoot.
Trying hard to get it right,
My dog thinks it's a frightful sight.

Perhaps a kazoo's the way to go,
But that might just steal the show.
Swinging wildly, off the beat,
Life's melody tastes like a treat.

Threads of Fate Intertwined

Knitting scarves with yarn so bright,
Each stitch a hope, a quirky sight.
Did I just add a sock or two?
Oh dear, what a silly view!

The threads they tangle in delight,
As I ponder if it's day or night.
With every twist, I find a clue,
But alas, it's just my kitten's shoe.

Mapping the Lost Pathways

I once misplaced my socks, so bright,
They vanished from my drawer one night.
I scoured the house, I checked the fridge,
I blamed the cat, she laughed, what a gig.

In every corner, I would peek,
Under the couch, that sneaky sneak.
Perhaps they took a trip away,
To sunny shores, to play all day.

I left a note, with cookies too,
Dear socks, we miss you, where are you?
But all I got was silence back,
Except for crumbs, a little snack.

So here I stand, with mismatched feet,
In a sockless world, I face the heat.
White with polka dots, a fashion sin,
Who knew lost socks could cause such din?

Quest for the Unwritten Chapter

Once I lost my pen, what a shame,
It ran away to play a game.
It inked a novel, I bet it did,
While I just searched, a bit more hid.

Pages blank, my ideas flew,
As the pen churned tales, just like stew.
I thought, 'what if it found its voice?'
While I just sighed, with no choice.

So I bought a pencil, sharp and bright,
To narrate dreams in the starry night.
Yet it crumbled, graphite spilled,
I grabbed a crayon, my fate was sealed.

Now my story's a colorful mess,
With stick figures in a fancy dress.
Who needs a pen's unwritten art?
When crayons bring the fun to heart!

Silent Yearnings of the Heart

In my chest beats a quiet drum,
For pizza cravings, I feel so numb.
An empty fridge, what could be worse?
I dream of cheese, my universe.

I scouted stores, with hope ablaze,
Found veggies there, in a giant maze.
I tried to cook, it fell apart,
Now veggie mush has gained my heart.

Yet in my dreams, a slice appears,
With pepperoni and cheesy cheers.
I take a bite, the flavors dance,
But here's the catch: I'm in a trance.

Behind the cravings, a funny tale,
In pursuit of snacks, I'll never fail.
So if you hear my belly growl,
Send pizza quick, it's time to howl!

Illuminating the Unlit Corners

In the shadows there's a sock, I swear,
Just last week, it wasn't there.
Who lit the dark and made it roam?
Is it searching, or just lost at home?

I grabbed a flashlight, all aglow,
To trace the path where dust bunnies go.
I stumbled on an old game piece,
And kitchen spices that haunt my peace.

Behind the couch, a treasure lies,
A forgotten remote, what a surprise!
I danced with glee, but who could've guessed,
Lost goods can lead to life's wild fest.

Now I embrace those hidden finds,
Quirky corners that free our minds.
Searching for laughs, in nooks and seams,
Is where we find our funniest dreams!

Unraveling Threads of Meaning

In a world of mismatched socks,
I hunt for what truly rocks.
These missing bits, they tease my mind,
Like puzzle pieces, hard to find.

I tried to glue my sandwich tight,
Thought it was love, but it was blight.
A cat that dances in my chair,
Still, no clue why I despair!

So many forks upon my plate,
Guess it's time to speculate.
Lost my marbles in the fray,
Where's the joy? It went to play!

With every step, I trip and trip,
On this wild, zany, cosmic trip.
Am I the joke or is it fate?
One thing's sure, life's never late!

In Search of the Lost Key

I misplaced my one true key,
It would unlock my sanity.
I checked the fridge and found some guac,
But where's the key? Just a sad shock!

I asked the cat if he had seen,
He just yawned, that little fiend.
The couch turned pirate, ate my stuff,
Is this key search really tough?

Under cushions, in the drawer,
Found a rubber chicken, not much more.
I guess I'll dance to my own beat,
As I search for something sweet!

The world's a treasure, quirky and wide,
With jigsaw pieces set aside.
Here's a laugh, let's have some fun,
Who knew life could be such a pun?

Whispers of the Incomplete Heart

My heart's a puzzle, edges torn,
A three-legged chair, forever worn.
I spin in circles, search for clues,
Where did I misplace my views?

In coffee cups and cereal bowls,
I sift for love amidst my scrolls.
A heart-shaped sticker, what's this stuff?
Is this enough, or crazy tough?

A wandering mind can paint a scene,
But finding joy? That's quite routine!
I chase my thoughts like butterflies,
But all I catch are silly cries.

So here I am, a puzzle piece,
With laughter, I'll find my release.
In this splendid, quirky art,
I'll mend the whispers of my heart!

Searching for Light Among Shadows

In shadows deep, where giggles creep,
I journey far, but then I leap.
I find a lamp, it's out of juice,
Just my luck, what a sad moose!

With every giggle, up I spring,
Searching for that stubborn zing.
The moon is laughing at my plight,
As I wander through the night.

Bright ideas dance like fireflies,
But why's my bread ate by the pies?
I'll chase the light until I see,
The laughter that's inside of me!

So let us twirl with shadows bright,
And bring more joy into the night.
For every laugh is sheer delight,
In this wild play of dark and light!

In Pursuit of Forgotten Dreams

In a land where socks run away,
And toast lands butter-side down,
I chase after dreams like a dog,
That's found a mysterious bone.

With giant cats that wear strange hats,
And fish that sing in the rain,
I ask the clouds where joy is hid,
But they just float and complain.

A map in hand, with doodles and plans,
Led me to a garden of socks,
Where fairies dance and giggle loud,
While I trip over boxes and rocks.

But in this chase, I find some grace,
In all the laughter and fun,
For maybe the dreams I think I seek,
Are hiding where the silliness runs.

Echoes of a Silent Desire

Whispers float on a crowded street,
Where pigeons gather in a dance,
Perhaps my heart's a vacant seat,
Waiting for love's goofy chance.

I survey the coffee shop line,
Hoping for more than a brew,
But the barista's got a wild eye,
And spills my latte, oh boo-hoo.

A fortune cookie cracks too late,
Proclaiming, 'Seek your heart's delight',
But I'm lost in a maze of fate,
Chasing after what feels right.

As echoes ring through streets so wide,
I trip on dreams and silly signs,
Yet in the missteps, I abide,
For laughter's found in tangled lines.

Seeking the Elusive Truth

In the library of unlearned facts,
I search for wisdom wrapped in cheer,
But every book's a riddle stacked,
Like pancakes without any syrup near.

The wise owl hoots in a comical way,
And winks an eye at my grand quest,
I ask for truths, he begins to sway,
And offers me a riddle as a jest.

With a magnifying glass, I inspect my tea,
Hoping to find the secret blend,
But all I gather is a honeybee,
And a lemon that wants to befriend.

Perhaps the truth's a silly game,
Disguised as fun filled with glee,
For in the chaos, I find my aim,
Is laughter, not clarity, you see!

Threads of the Unconnected

I gather stray threads from my old clothes,
To stitch a story that makes me grin,
But every time I start to pose,
The needle jumps, and I can't begin.

Mixing patterns that don't quite match,
Like kittens trying to dance a jig,
I create a quilt that's quite a catch,
Full of patches both small and big.

Each loop and knot a silly tale,
Of misfit socks and wandering shoes,
With every tug, I hope to unveil,
The bright side of my knitting blues.

For in this tapestry I weave,
I find a joy that's pure and bright,
A reminder that in all we believe,
It's the quirks that give life its light.

Unfinished Stories in the Wind

Once upon a time, I lost my shoe,
Chasing dreams that just wouldn't do.
They laugh, they tease, 'Where's your pair?'
I shrug, I grin, with wind-blown hair.

My cat wears shades, struts with pride,
Trying to find where the sun hides.
If life's a joke, I'm missing the punch,
Just looking for laughs with my lunchtime crunch.

Clues Beneath the Surface

I dug a hole in search of gold,
Found an old sock, now that's bold!
The map was drawn by a toddler's hand,
X marks the spot, or so they planned.

A bottle cap is now my crown,
In this treasure hunt, I won't frown.
Sifting through sand for a breadcrumb trail,
Who knew clues could be so very frail?

Navigating the Maze of Existence

I ventured forth, coffee in hand,
Lost in a maze, it's not quite grand.
Walls are sticky, paths are long,
Is that a hint, or just my song?

Ducking under, hopping over,
Turns out, I'm more lost than a rover.
With a goofy grin, I can't help but laugh,
Stumbling through life on my funky path.

The Dance of Missing Elements

In a waltz with socks, one vanished away,
Twirl with the broom, it's a sweeping ballet.
The fridge hums a tune, the light starts to dance,
While I search for my keys, will they take a chance?

Laughter erupts when I trip on the mat,
Did I step on my dreams, or just the cat?
In this frolicsome jig, I'm just trying to see,
What fun little wonders await in the spree!

The Scent of Forgotten Possibilities

In the attic of thoughts, they hide,
Old socks and dreams, side by side.
Where's that thought I tossed away?
Maybe in the laundry today?

I sniff the air, a mystery breeze,
Is it lost hopes or just old cheese?
A whiff of joy, a hint of glee,
Or just the cat? Oh, let it be!

Uncovering the Hidden Facet

With a shovel and a quirky grin,
I dig for laughter buried in.
What gems await in this quest of mine?
Perhaps a sock or a half-used brine?

Oh look, a coin from '84,
And a rubber duck that quacks for more!
Each flip reveals a silly pie,
Why did I dig? Oh, well, I'll try!

The Elixir of Completion

A potion brewed with thoughts unmet,
Stir sure, but don't spill a bit yet!
A dash of joy, a sprinkle of fun,
And maybe just one more pun!

Could this be the magic to make it whole?
Or just another mishap, bless my soul!
I'll sip and dance on this crazy spree,
Take a selfie with my missing G!

Beyond the Horizon of Dreams

I sail my ship of whimsical plans,
Navigating seas where humor spans.
Past jellyfish and floating pies,
Searching for laughs in starry skies.

There's treasure chests with jokes inside,
And silly hats that tickle and glide.
Each wave a quip, each breeze a jest,
In the ocean of dreams, we jest the best!

The Undiscovered Note

In a symphony of socks so mismatched,
A lonely note fell, feeling detached.
It craves a tune, but hums like a fool,
Dancing atop a forgotten stool.

Cats in the corner, they plot and they scheme,
Chasing that note in a whimsical dream.
The violin sighs, the trumpet just moans,
While the world spins 'round like a juggler's cones.

Lost Symbols of Existence

In a land where hieroglyphs laugh and play,
Missing their meanings, they've gone astray.
A smiley face drawn on an ancient stone,
Curses the scholars who stand all alone.

With a wink and a nod, they scribble away,
Trying to decode the bad hierarchy ballet.
But who needs a lesson when puns rule the day,
And lost symbols giggle, saying, "We're here to stay!"

The Taste of Unfinished Dreams

A recipe lost in a fog of delight,
With sprinkles of whimsy and giggles in sight.
The cake looks confused with frosting that's blue,
While it wonders aloud, "What am I meant to do?"

The spoon took a chance and leaped on the floor,
Screaming, "I'm just here for a bit of rapport!"
But dreams have no flavors when baked half-cocked,
Only crumbs of confusion, newly mocked.

Edge of the Unknown

On the brink of absurdity, humor abounds,
With creatures in costumes performing their rounds.
A penguin in shades took a seat with a drink,
And offered a jellyfish some time for a wink.

They pondered together, what's missing today,
Maybe a punchline to liven the gray?
As stars started twinkling, they danced on the line,
Of the edge of the unknown, feeling just fine.

Fragments of a Wholeness

I lost a puzzle piece today,
Underneath my cat's ballet.
It's hiding with the socks, I swear,
Or stuck in Mom's old comfy chair.

My jigsaw dreams now look so bare,
With corners missing, time to spare.
I shake the box, what do I find?
Just crumbs and one old grapevine rind.

Quest for the Unseen Corner

I sought a corner, seemingly tight,
Yet found my sandwich, what a fright!
Tuna, lettuce, all in the mix,
Room for more? Add a few tricks!

Each twist and turn, a piece amiss,
Where can it be? I ponder this.
Then laughter strikes as I behold,
A taco shell, so brave and bold!

Echoes of an Unfinished Tapestry

My tapestry hangs, a sight to see,
With colors bright, a mystery.
But wait, what's this? A hole so wide,
Where's that fabric I planned to hide?

The dog's been rummaging around,
Leaving threads lost on the ground.
I laugh and sigh, for what's the use?
I'll frame it now, call it "loose truce!"

The Longing for Wholeness

I sought completion, pieced it right,
But ended up with a furry fright.
My pieces scattered far and wide,
Beneath the couch, where dust bunnies hide.

In every nook, I search and muse,
Imagine I'll find my friend's old shoes.
Yet laughter rings, they're not my fate,
A half-baked cookie is my plate!

Unfolding the Mystery of Us

In a box of forgotten socks,
   Our clues are in the lint.
With a magnifying glass, we probe,
   Have you seen my lost mint?

We chase around the cat's lost toy,
   While giggling 'til we cry.
Every detour brings a new joy,
   Like a pizza pie that's high.

The jigsaw puzzles stacked so high,
   Where edges look like fruit.
We laugh at shapes that don't comply,
   Like trying to knit a boot!

Together we will turn around,
   In circles, we will dance.
Hilarious, our lives resound,
   To find that missing chance!

Patching Quilts of Time

With scraps of life and threads of cheer,
    We stitch our tale so bright.
Grandma's quilt is filled with fear,
    That our parties end at night.

Each patch a memory so delight,
    From picnics in the sun.
We argue 'bout the colors right,
    'Til we laugh and call it fun!

A tape measure's tangled mess,
    That no one knew was there.
We count our blunders, I confess,
    While dodging Dad's bold glare.

Yet in the chaos, joy we find,
    As stitches twist and turn.
In every quilt, our hearts entwined,
    For laughter, we all yearn!

Pieces of a Dream Yet Unfound

In a land where socks come alive,
They dance and sing on floor.
A puzzle here, a riddle sly,
What's behind that closet door?

We search for keys beneath the couch,
The remote, it does a waltz.
With giggles high, we start to crouch,
Blaming squirrels for our faults.

The map is drawn in crayon hues,
Detailing snacks and fun.
Each X marks a wild goose,
So just stay away from the bun!

But what we find is pure delight,
In every laugh, a clue.
We may be lost but spirits bright,
Our fun is just for two!

The Pursuit of Hidden Whimsy

In quest of socks that disappear,
We ride a kangaroo.
Through laundry fields, we persevere,
And giggle at the view.

Our treasure map's a cereal box,
With marshmallows for bait.
Through jungles made of cat's hard knocks,
We search for something great.

The joy we find is quite absurd,
Like cheese that sings a tune.
With whispers of a silly word,
We'll dance beneath the moon.

For in this hunt, we valiant chase,
The whimsies that make us cheer.
Through every bend, we share this space,
Together we'll hold dear!

The Unraveling of Deep Questions

Why's a chicken crossing the road,
Do we need its code to crack?
Is there purpose in each tick and tock,
Or just a snack we lack?

Do ducks wear hats when they quack,
Is the moon just a giant pie?
Beneath the stars, we swear to ask,
Before we bid the day goodbye.

Why do socks vanish in the wash,
Are they off to a secret land?
With crayons and glue, we might too,
If only we could understand.

So let's raise our glasses, cheers to fun,
And ponder these puzzling ways.
In laughter we'll find some missing bits,
To fill our quirky days.

Where Pieces Long to Align

In a drawer where odd socks hide,
Is there a puzzle piece or two?
Maybe they sneaked out with pride,
To find a match, that's true.

Why do spatulas have their quirks,
And spoons prefer to glide?
Perhaps they're seeking wacky perks,
In the cutlery's great divide.

A fork with dreams of being a knife,
Chasing the thrill of the slice.
Or a spoon wishing for a singer's life,
In a concert full of rice.

Let's gather 'round and bring them near,
These missing bits of lore.
Together we'll laugh and cheer,
As they dance forevermore.

Seeking the Heartbeat of Existence

In a blender whirring thoughts away,
    What pulses beneath the skin?
Is it laughter, love, or just a play,
    Of all the quirks within?

The toaster pops with hope and cheer,
    As crumbs fly left and right.
Could that be the happy gear,
    In our quest for delight?

What if ants have secret chats,
    But can't find a proper phone?
While caterpillars don silly hats,
    And giggle when alone.

Come gather 'round, let's have a blast,
    With giggles and silly tales.
As we bounce from present to the past,
    To uncover hidden trails.

The Lure of Untold Stories

What tales do cereal boxes hold,
If only they could chat?
In the shadows, secrets unfold,
Where do those marshmallows pat?

Every fridge hums a quiet song,
Of pickles and pasta dreams.
Are we missing the gist for long,
In hunt for playful schemes?

Do walls whisper ancient lore,
Of dance parties unseen?
Each corner, a spin and a roar,
Of legacies untouched, serene.

So let's dive in and share a laugh,
At stories yet to be penned.
With every giggle, we'll carve a path,
To where the fun won't end.

The Unsolved Enigma of Being

In a world of mismatched socks,
I ponder my purpose and thoughts.
Is it coffee or cake that brings joy?
Maybe I'm just a lost little toy.

I asked a squirrel about my aim,
He just laughed and called me lame.
Chasing shadows, I spin around,
In this circus, I'm the clown unbound.

A frog serenades me with his croak,
I chuckle at life, what a great joke!
While kittens plot a world takeover,
I'm still here, finding my four-leaf clover.

What's missing? A hat or a shoe?
Or maybe it's just old déjà vu.
With each laugh and quirky misstep,
I find pieces to my jigsaw prep.

Threads of Destiny Awaiting

I threaded a needle with dreams of gold,
Yet all I sewed were stories untold.
A cat walked in like she owns the place,
While my visions of grandeur just lost their grace.

A pizza slice offered me wisdom deep,
"Don't overthink, just take a leap!"
But then it felt like a cheesy trap,
So I leaned back and took a nap.

With fortunes written on fortune fries,
I dipped in ketchup, took a bite, surprise!
The universe giggled at my plight,
As I searched for meaning with all my might.

Each thread I pulled made more knots arise,
Like socks enchanted to play hide-and-seek spies.
But one day I'll stitch this crazy quilt,
And find life's thread, where dreams are built.

Scattered Visions of Unity

I spied a puzzle, bits in a pot,
Colors and shapes, but the edges are hot.
A turtle named Larry offered advice,
"Take your time, and you might find it nice!"

With crayons scattered across the floor,
I drew a sun, then forgot what it's for.
Aliens called me via hotdog phone,
"Stop looking for pieces, just come to our zone!"

A robot danced, with moves all askew,
While I tripped over my own shoe.
Unity sparkled like glitter in air,
But I forgot what I was meant to wear.

As I gathered gems from under my bed,
I thought of laughter and things left unsaid.
In this quest so absurd, yet real,
I find joy in all these odd spins of the wheel.

The Journey to Find Missing Colors

In my quest for hues, I lost my brush,
Colors swirled in a wacky rush.
Like a parrot stuck on repeat,
I painted the sky with a polka-dot beat.

A rainbow told me to stay away,
"Mixing colors might ruin my display!"
But with every splash, I danced in the rain,
Color-blind squirrels joined me in refrain.

I found a paint can with shades divine,
But the lid laughed at me, said, "Read the sign!"
"Stay within the lines," but I felt too wild,
So I sprayed some laughter, like an exuberant child.

With every misstep and splash I made,
I stitched a quilt that would never fade.
In this kaleidoscope of all that I see,
I gave life a hug, just let it be free.

Whispers of the Unfound

I looked for clues in my sock drawer,
But all I found were socks galore.
A note said, "Check under your bed!"
But just some dust bunnies danced instead.

My cat keeps staring at the wall,
Is she plotting my next great fall?
I asked her for wisdom, she just yawned,
As if my musings were all but pawned.

The neighbor's dog barks out a tune,
While I search for answers beneath the moon.
A sandwich half-eaten sits on my plate,
Perhaps it holds wisdom—wait, is that fate?

So, off I go on this wild goose chase,
Chasing my thoughts at a dizzying pace.
If laughter's the key to life's missing part,
Then maybe I'll find it right here, in my heart!

Chasing Shadows of Purpose

In my backyard, a gnome gives a wink,
Does he know the answers, or just like to drink?
He points to a map made of cheese and pie,
But all it leads to is a blurry sky!

I grabbed my magnifying glass for a peek,
Excitedly searching—I'm feeling quite chic.
A squirrel steals my compass, runs up a tree,
Now I'm lost and my map looks like Swiss cheese!

I once found a key beneath my old hat,
Turns out it unlocked the door to my cat.
With laughter, I greeted the feline surprise,
She's the real explorer with mischievous eyes.

So here I am, with a to-do list long,
Chasing shadows while humming a tune, oh so wrong.
If zest is the puzzle piece I can score,
Then turn up the laughter, and let's find some more!

Fragments of a Hidden Truth

I stumbled upon a dusty book,
Its title was strange, so I took a look.
It spoke of pirates and treasure so grand,
But all I found was a rubber band!

In a cereal box, I discovered a clue,
A tiny note read, "Try something new."
I poured out the Cheerios and found a toy,
A miniature car, oh what a joy!

A fortune cookie crumbled in my hand,
Said, "Life's discovery is cleverly planned."
I cracked it open with hopeful delight,
Only to find—oh, a chicken's plight!

So off I wander, with giggles and quirks,
Searching for wisdom in dances of jerks.
If laughter's the thread of this riddle divine,
Then I'll stitch together these fragments of mine!

The Hunt for Harmony's Key

I checked my fridge for some ancient cheese,
Hoping its wisdom would help me with ease.
A pickle jar whispered, "Try dancing instead!"
And suddenly chaos reigned in my head!

I spun and I twirled right over the cat,
Who looked unimpressed, and just sat on my hat.
"Perhaps I should stick to the rhythm of grace,"
But you should see how I waddle in place!

A rubber duckie joined on my quest,
With a quack and a splash, it truly impressed.
Together we laughed, as we searched high and low,
For life's missing piece in a most silly show.

So if harmony's key is a jolly old trick,
I'll look for it here, in a dance or a flick.
Come join this madcap, delightful parade,
In the quest for the laughter many have made!

The Unraveled Map of the Soul

My map's a scribble, not a guide,
It leads to places where socks collide.
X marks the spot, but it's a tease,
I find a sandwich, oh, where's my keys?

Exploring towns that don't exist,
I lose my way, I think I missed.
With every turn, it gets more wild,
I hear a cow moo, like a lost child.

I penned my dreams in a coffee cup,
But all it holds is cold, old slurp.
My soul's treasure map, a funny riddle,
With every "Here" I find a middle.

So grab your hat, let's spin around,
The hidden piece is where it's found.
Just laugh, my friend, don't take it tough,
The journey's fun, and that's enough!

Sifting Through the Sands of Meaning

I'm at the beach, with thoughts like sand,
Each grain's a giggle, a half-formed plan.
I sift for thoughts, but all I find,
Are crabs that dance and shells unkind.

My bucket's filled with odd desires,
A sunburnt nose and broken wires.
The compass spins without a course,
My ice cream melts, oh what a force!

With every wave, I lose my clue,
What does it mean? I haven't a view.
I build a castle, but it falls flat,
Just a sandy mound, hey, where's the cat?

So let's rejoice in this sandy mess,
As we find joy in the search, no stress.
The meaning's found in laughter shared,
In every silly wave we dared!

Journeying Through the Void

In the void I wander, feeling quite light,
Floating through space, it's a comical sight.
I trip on stardust and giggle with glee,
Are those meteors or just flies near me?

I ask the cosmos where to go next,
It responds with laughter, oh, what a text!
With each twisted turn, I lose my way,
But find a donut, hey, I'll stay!

Galaxies swirl like a dance-off scene,
I'm just a jester in a wobbly machine.
With each spinning star, my worries dissolve,
In this great void, there's much to solve!

So come float by, let's have some fun,
In the endless sky, we'll get stuff done.
We're searching for pieces, but let's face facts,
The joy is the journey, not all the cracks!

Quest for the Unseen Fragment

I searched high and low for that missing piece,
In the fridge last seen—what a funny feast!
Between the carrots and the old cheese wheel,
I found a pickle! Oh, how surreal!

With a magnifying glass, I scoured the floor,
Under the sofa—what's that, more gore?
Old socks and crumbs, my treasure trove,
I'm a pirate now, with no place to stow!

The sock goblin laughs as I scratch my head,
Maybe I lost it while making my bed?
I'm slinging pillows like they're soft bricks,
Dreaming of finding my puzzle mix.

So join me, friend, in this zany chase,
Each lost fragment adds to the grace.
We'll laugh and trip, come take a chance,
In this quest, let's just dance!

Paths of the Uncertain Traveler

With map in hand, I wander wide,
The signs are blurred, I take a ride.
A left, a right, then a big ol' flop,
Is this the top or the bottom of the shop?

I ask a cat where I should stray,
It winks at me then walks away.
A squirrel chimes in, full of delight,
"Just keep going, you'll be all right!"

Got shoes on wrong, I trip and fall,
But every tumble, I hear a call.
The birds serenade me, out of tune,
Finding my way beneath the moon.

So here I am, a traveler lost,
Collecting thoughts, forgetting the cost.
With laughter loud, I'll make my way,
Life's a game, come what may!

The Dance of Lost Connections

I tried to reach you through my phone,
But all it gave me was a tone.
"Can you hear me now?" I loudly cried,
Yet all I got was dropped and fried.

The Wi-Fi signal waved goodbye,
When I needed it most, oh my, oh my!
I danced the jig with my lost texts,
An awkward move, what is next?

I googled hotlines, followed trends,
But every number just pretends.
The only voice was my own despair,
As pizza rolled in, I tried to share.

So here I sit, a techy fool,
With empty screens and no way to drool.
In this dance of lost electric sparks,
I twirl and laugh like I had some quarks!

Shadows Searching for Light

In the corner, shadows creep,
Whispering secrets, oh so deep.
One says, "Hey, let's take a hike!"
The other chuckles, "Not tonight!"

They stumble over silent rocks,
Tripping on time, avoiding clocks.
"Hey, where's the glow?" one shadow shouts,
The other rolls eyes, and pouts and doubts.

Through alleyways and dusty scenes,
They search for dreams in faded jeans.
Yet light is there, just out of reach,
Like a beach-ball game with a sneaky peach.

So on they go, these silly frames,
Chasing glimmers, playing games.
Shadows at play, they'll never bite,
In a world where darkness meets the light!

Unwritten Stories of the Heart

Pages blank, I skip and hop,
Finding tales that make me stop.
With doodles here and scribbles there,
Each moment a story, light as air.

An old shoe waits by the door,
It holds the dreams of days before.
With every scuff, a laugh ensues,
A million thoughts and happy blues.

The cat wants cuddles, the dog wants play,
While my heart writes poetry every day.
Each moment savored, a little clue,
Of what life's story wants to view.

So here I sit, with pen in hand,
Not quite sure of where I stand.
Yet I know each line will come to start,
In unwritten stories of the heart!

The Puzzle of Existence

In a box of jumbled parts,
I found a shoe and three blue hearts.
Oh what fun, this messy spree,
Where's the piece that looks like me?

A corner snug, a flat edge wide,
With chocolate stains I cannot hide.
I check the dog, I check the cat,
They just stare back; imagine that!

Under cushions, behind the chair,
Everywhere, but is it fair?
To find a piece that fits my groove,
And build a game to make me move!

Maybe it's an alien prank,
Or the mailman's secret prankster rank.
I'll grab some friends, we'll solve with glee,
Who knew life's work could be so free?

Navigating the Labyrinth of Longing

In a maze with walls so tall,
I tripped on nothing, started to crawl.
Where's the exit? Where's the flow?
Just my sandwich and a lost toe!

Maps are fuzzy, cheese is near,
I asked a squirrel, but he just sneered.
With crumbs to guide, I'll find the way,
To a treasure trove of jokes and play!

Twists and turns all lead astray,
A donut shop? I'll just stay.
Eating sprinkles, laughing loud,
Who knew lost pieces came in a crowd?

I might just sit, not move ahead,
With frosting dreams, who needs to tread?
In this labyrinth of endless fun,
Life's real puzzle has just begun!

Searching for the Golden Thread

With scissors out, I look for gold,
Threads of laughter, the stories told.
My grandma's quilt, some socks askew,
I knot them tight, a wacky crew!

Tangled yarns that lead astray,
Bring me joy, come what may.
I find a shoe, a rubber duck,
Stitching chaos—oh what luck!

A rainbow seemed to stretch so wide,
But all I got was a toenail guide.
I'll sew together bits of cheer,
And wear my weirdness loud and clear!

Who needs a plan, or world so bright,
When ties of laughter make it right?
With each tangle, a story we weave,
In the fabric of life, I believe.

The Invisible Link

I sought a connecting piece so sly,
In avocado's pit, and the pie in the sky.
Invisible links, oh what a tease,
Like finding socks in a windstorm breeze!

Rummaging through the attic's maze,
Found a note marked with "no ways."
Chasing shadows, laughing bright,
Where's that link to my delight?

With glitter glue and a rubber band,
I crafted things that no one planned.
Singing loudly, I hope to find,
Connections lost—are they so blind?

In a world of misfits, I'll take my stand,
With a wink and grin, isn't life grand?
The invisible threads weave in and out,
In laughter, connection, there's no doubt!

Beyond the Boundless Abyss

In a world of socks, one is shy,
Hiding behind the couch, oh my!
It wanders off, seeking to flee,
While I just want a pair, you see.

Lost keys laugh from under the bed,
Distant giggles of bread rolls, unsaid.
They plot to make my mornings a mess,
Ode to chaos, oh how they impress!

The cat brings back the wrong toy mouse,
A feathery thing from the neighbor's house.
I scratch my head, as she prances around,
Her puzzled expression, utterly profound.

Maybe a clue's in the fridge,
Next to the milk, perched on the ridge.
A note from the broccoli, hefty and green,
It claims it's the king, if you know what I mean!

Unraveling the Enigma Within

A puzzle piece rolled under the stairs,
Snickering softly, causing affairs.
It giggles like it knows it's the one,
But why is it hiding? Oh, what fun!

A cookie jar whispers, 'Let us feast!'
In crumbly chaos, I am the least.
Each reach yields a cookie and a flop,
How did I end up with the bottom drop?

The dog's got a sock, he thinks it's a toy,
He wags it around with innocent joy.
While I search for sanity, lost in the haze,
He's busy creating mischief-filled days.

To the attic I go, climbing each rung,
A banjo sings out, it's not even strung.
This odd little tune plays with such flair,
Found my missing piece? Nah, just an old chair!

Questing for the Lost Connection

Balloons float high, all lost in the sky,
One dreams of adventure, oh me, oh my!
Chasing the breeze with an untied string,
Planned for a party, but off it did spring.

Beneath the couch lives a villainous sock,
With tales of mischief around every block.
It trips my toes while I'm on a roll,
Should have been a hero, it plays the poll.

What's that buzzing? A bee with a grin,
Adventuring in circles, it "tum-tum-tums" in.
I try to escape but it seems to insist,
On joining my quest; really hard to resist!

A search for a charger ends with a nudge,
Found a hairbrush, does it bear a grudge?
What a wild path of detours and laughs,
Maybe the journey's the best; what a gaffe!

The Yearning for Wholeness

In the kitchen a spatula splats,
Dancing with joy, while a pot just chats.
The forks and knives hold a banquet so bold,
Plans of a party, or so it is told!

A wayward lid goes a-rollin' away,
Hiding from pans, oh, what a good play!
The sugar jar giggles, all frosted in glee,
While spoons form a band with a teapot decree.

Tangled up cables that think they're a snake,
Playing hide and seek, make no mistake.
I battle, I wrestle, but they win again,
Oh, tech may be smart, but all we need's zen!

A broken chair asks, "Who needs a leg?"
With laughter and splinters, how can one beg?
Perhaps I'll just join in this wacky parade,
For in silly chaos, life's truly laid!

The Hunt for Invisible Threads

In a quest for a thing that we can't even see,
I checked the fridge and the garden tree.
A sock in the dryer, my lost TV remote,
With a broken compass, I sail this odd boat.

I asked a goldfish if it could lend a clue,
It just swam in circles, as most fish do.
My cat held a conference, all paws and no words,
While I searched for answers in chirps of the birds.

A map made of jellybeans, I actually tried,
To find where they sell the most baffling guide.
I tripped over laughter, I stumbled on glee,
In this wild treasure hunt, I'm lost, but so free!

With a query so silly, I'll surely land gold,
In this quest of the quirky, the brave, and the bold.
Like a muffin that's missing its sweet, cherry top,
My search is hilarious, and it just won't stop!

In Quest of the Last Element

With a beaker of chaos and a dash of some flair,
I searched for an element, up in the air.
A sprinkle of nonsense, a pinch of delight,
In my lab, there's laughter that takes to new heights.

I mixed up some candy with powder and goo,
Expecting a miracle - only got stew!
The periodic table? A riddle to crack,
When sodium's winking and argon's laid back.

An inkblot of wonder, a twist in my fate,
I asked my pet hamster - it snoozed, it was late.
The last element, surely it hides among socks,
And the pop-tarts that vanished, oh what a paradox!

Stripping logic bare, I dance on my chair,
In a quest for the missing, with no time to spare.
With giggles as goggles and quirks on my side,
I know that in laughter, true treasures collide!

Canvas of a Fractured Dream

On a canvas of chaos, I dabble with fate,
My brush strokes of whimsy, they fluctuate.
Lost pieces are hiding in splatters of cream,
Somewhere in this madness, awaits my true dream.

Each color a giggle, each line is a jest,
I paint with my whims, oh what a wild quest!
Like a cat with a crayon, I scribble and sigh,
In this fractured puzzle, oh me, oh my!

The blue paints a turtle that thinks it can fly,
While the orange holds secrets that whisper and cry.
There's a touch of confetti, a splash of bright laugh,
I'm lost in creation, this absurd craft!

When the sun takes a bow and the moon starts to scheme,

I'll find that lost puzzle - or maybe I'll dream.
In the laughter of colors, I'll surely find peace,
For a canvas of folly is where joys increase!

Gathering Starlit Memories

Under a sky where the giggles collide,
I'm gathering stardust with laughter as my guide.
A constellation of quirky, with bright shiny bits,
I collect all the chuckles that life often flits.

With a jar full of moments, I twirl in delight,
I'll catch all the snickers that float through the night.
A tickle from twilight, a nudge from the dawn,
In this whimsical treasure, my worries are gone.

Each star beams a jest, each memory spins,
While the moon giggles softly, with playful grins.
I hitch a ride on a comet, that's laden with cheer,
Shouting "Here I am, oh funny life, dear!"

So let's dance through the cosmos, with mirth in the air,
As I gather the memories, scattered with care.
For in every small giggle and starlit embrace,
I find all the pieces, in joy's warm embrace!

The Quest for a Harmonious Whole

In a world of mismatched socks,
I seek the shoe that truly rocks.
A left with a right, oh what a bliss,
But all I find is this strange abyss.

I've tried a puzzle full of cheese,
But mice got to it, if you please!
They nibbled corners, ate the peas,
And left me with crumbs, oh, such unease!

A cat once claimed my shiny piece,
It curled up, and slept in peace.
I found a rubber duck to keep,
But quacking dreams just made me weep.

With a laugh, I search the park,
Oh where's the piece that will ignite a spark?
Chasing rainbows and pizza crust,
Who knew this quest was just a bust?

Disconnected Yet Yearning

I lost my marbles in the fray,
A game of life, where I can't play.
Searching for that one last round,
Are they hiding where I can't be found?

With every giggle, my heart takes flight,
Yet jigsaw pieces are out of sight.
Found a clue in a cereal box,
But all that's there are sneaky flocks!

My goldfish gave up, swam in circles,
As I pondered my missing hurdles.
A search for fun, with a twist of fate,
The treasure map's just a dinner plate!

Disconnected hearts, they laugh and sing,
While I search for a lighthearted thing.
The puzzle's a joke, so wild and free,
Join me in this quirky spree!

Unveiling the Silent Yearning

Oh why is my sandwich missing a slice?
A lettuce leaf that'd be so nice!
Took a walk down Silly Street,
Found a squirrel with my lost treat!

Whispers of snacks float through the air,
Desires so loud, it's simply unfair.
Yet the silence of crumbs brings a grin,
I dance with my mismatched shoes of kin!

A tangle of wires, they form a maze,
And I stand here in a daze.
Seeking cables that don't misbehave,
But they jump around like they're trying to rave!

In this quirky life of twists and bends,
I'll keep searching for my quirky friends.
Each giggle and chuckle adds to my quest,
Who knew the hunt could be such a jest?

Shadowed Journey of the Soul

In search of a sock that feels just right,
I tripped on the cat in the middle of night.
She swiped my dreams with a flick of her tail,
Echoed laughter, the cat's holy grail!

My heart's like a puzzle, a bit out of tune,
With pieces of laughter beneath the moon.
In corners of chaos, I can't help but grin,
Where lost are the pieces that whisk me within!

I wandered through shadows of mismatched shoes,
In hopes of a piece that could banish blues.
Yet to my surprise, it's the giggles I find,
Laughter's the magic that unites all kinds!

So here I stand, with joy in my stride,
In search of the piece that's my goofy guide.
Life's lovely mess is the fun I embrace,
As I dance through the shadows, I find my place!

The Fragmented Journey

I wandered through the cosmic mall,
Hoping to find my missing ball.
Salespeople laughed, they pointed keen,
'This ain't a puzzle, it's just cuisine!'

Socks with polka dots, hats so spry,
I slipped on a banana peel, oh my!
But as I rolled down the galaxy's track,
I realized maybe I had it all stacked.

Stars giggled as I tripped and fell,
As I searched for a clue from my own cell.
They said, 'Chase the comet that shows your spark,'
But does it wear a hat or just bark?

Through wormholes I twisted, I spun and swayed,
"Is that my piece?" I jokingly played.
Turns out my treasure was right under my nose,
A slice of pizza, and yes, it still glows!

Whispers Across Time and Space

In a cosmic café, they serve dreams,
I ordered a slice of life, it seems.
But when it came, it was cheese without,
Jesus, where's the pepperoni shout?

Aliens whispered, tucked behind a star,
'Look for the piece, yet it's not too far!'
I squinted at shadows, I knocked on wood,
Turns out it was my childhood, how very good!

A rocket-powered dog ran past a nebula,
Chasing space cats, oh how peculiar!
I chased them too, with hopes that they'd know,
Where the puzzle piece is, surely they'll show!

With laughter echoing through the vast unknown,
I gathered my whims, all frightfully grown.
In the end, the secret was light as a feather,
It's not about pieces, but the fun we gather!

Echoes of a Broken Heart

Once my heart did bounce like a ball,
'Til I lost it in a grocery stall.
The shoppers laughed, they pointed, oh dear,
'Your heart's on sale, but it's not quite clear!'

With breakups and mix-ups along my quest,
Valentine cards revealed my jest.
A heart-shaped cookie sent me in spins,
'Tis sugar I need, not these ol' sins!

In this scavenger hunt of love's charade,
I found some confetti amidst the charade.
With cupcakes galore, I threw a grand fête,
To celebrate bits of love, I won't forget!

So if you misplace your heart on a whim,
Just look for the pie, or a dance to begin.
If life throws you crumbs, make a sweet art,
Sometimes the best fit is a chocolate heart!

Searching for Infinity

I set off one day to find endless glee,
Frolicking freely, just me and my tea.
Infinity's charming, but where has it gone?
Maybe it's napping on a lawn's soft dawn!

Mathematical beings raised their brows high,
I asked for a hint while sipping my pie.
They chuckled and plotted with glee all around,
'Look for the pi; it's where fun can be found!'

With fractals and giggles, I twirled through the night,
Every corner I turned shimmered with light.
Yet as I twirled in the cosmic ballet,
I realized that laughter's infinity plays!

So here's to the journey, may it tickle your fate,
For sometimes the search has more than weight.
Infinity is joyful, not just one big plea,
It's the silly old dance, you shared with your tea!

The Call of the Uncharted

A map drawn in crayon, so bold and so bright,
Winding through gardens of pure delight.
X marks the spot where I lost my last shoe,
Chasing the treasure, oh what could it do?

Sailing on puddles, my ship made of leaves,
Finding the fortune that nobody believes.
A dragonfly whispered, 'Try not to fall,'
But I tripped on a daisy, oh how I did sprawl!

The compass is broken, spins wildly around,
Pointing to snacks and the softest of ground.
With each goofy giggle, adventure I seek,
In this fabulous quest, I find joy in the week.

So here I stand, with my hat full of dreams,
Catching some laughter along with the beams.
I'd trade it all for that one missing part,
But for now, it's the giggles that warm up my heart.

Journals of a Wayward Heart

Oh dear diary, today has been wild,
Met a squirrel who said he was once a child.
He offered me nuts, said I should be bold,
And follow my whims, for they're worth their weight in gold.

I tried to be brave, took off on a whim,
In search of a rhino, or maybe a him.
But all that I found was a zebra with style,
Who laughed and told stories that made me stay awhile.

The pages get thicker with mishaps and glee,
From singing with pigeons, to dancing with tea.
I scratched down my thoughts, not with pen, but with cheer,
In hopes that my heart may someday find its gear.

So here's to the journey, all quirky and bright,
With gumdrops and giggles and stars in the night.
My journal's a treasure, though it lacks a clear guide,
Yet the pages are bursting with love that can't hide.

The Shape of Longing

I once sought a donut, round as the moon,
But discovered a bagel, and hummed a new tune.
The shape was surprising, but I gave it a whirl,
With each bite I giggled, what a crazy swirl!

In a world full of angles, I craved something true,
A triangle sandwich just wouldn't do.
I searched for my gift wrapped in layers of fun,
But found silly hats resting under the sun.

Where is my piece that can fit in so neat?
Perhaps in a noodle or under a seat?
My heart does a tango, my soul starts to prance,
Finding pieces of joy in this whimsical dance.

So laugh with me now, as I look high and low,
For joy's in the journey, as we shimmy and flow.
With every odd shape I embrace with delight,
I find all the puzzles are sweetened by night.

Awakenings from the Abyss

In a world full of shadows, where socks like to flee,
I woke up one morning to find coffee with glee.
The monsters of chaos had kept me in fright,
But I found that they danced in the soft morning light.

With a yawn and a stretch, I decided to sing,
To scare off the fears and let giggles take wing.
I slipped on a banana, not one, but a fleet,
And fell, like a dancer, right down to my feet.

Now echoes of laughter swirl over the gloom,
As I twirl through the valleys where chaos would bloom.
A treasure unspotted, a pie in the sky,
In the very abyss, I found my supply.

So raise up your glasses, embrace every flaw,
For in silly missteps, there's wisdom we draw.
The puzzles of living may twist and may fray,
But it's laughter and love that brighten our day.

The Winds of Tempestuous Hope

In a land where socks go to hide,
A search for comfort we can't abide.
With mismatched patterns, we frolic and play,
Chasing that warmth that's gone astray.

Pants in the dryer, who knows their fate?
Could they be off, on a daring date?
We chuckle and ponder, while sipping our tea,
Maybe they found a new life, carefree!

With every lost item, a tale starts to form,
Of epic adventures, not quite the norm.
Like chewed-up shoes or a single glove,
Perhaps they're just seeking the things they love.

So we search with a grin and a whimsical twist,
For the missing pieces, that can't be missed.
A sock, a shoe, or a wayward hat,
In the end, they'll surely return; imagine that!

Threads of the Universe Unspooled

In the attic, all tangled and tight,
Yarns of the cosmos loom out of sight.
A needle enjoys its cosmic spree,
Stitching together a new galaxy!

Buttons and beads, a curious crew,
Every stitch whispers a secret or two.
With each little knot, we laugh and we cheer,
For lost threads find ways to reappear.

Measuring life with a tape of pure whim,
Sewing and laughing with joy on a whim.
We'll patch up the universe, all sewn with grace,
Till we spot that one piece, lost in outer space.

So grab that ol' thread, and mend the divine,
In this wacky patchwork, we joyfully twine.
The universe giggles with cosmic delight,
As we channel our fun into the endless night.

In Pursuit of the Divine Pin

In a drawer of chaos, a pin waits to shine,
Like it's been on vacation, sipping on brine.
Searching for something it might never find,
An elusive adventure, oh isn't it kind?

With pencils and paper, we craft a grand map,
To hunt for that pin, while we giggle and flap.
On a quest through the fridge, the couch, and the car,
Who knew a small pin could travel so far?

Through rain and through shine, we chase it with glee,
"Where are you, dear pin?" cries our puzzled decree.
In the chaos of life, it's a funny old game,
To find that small treasure and call out its name.

And when we finally spot it, gleaming with pride,
We pop the champagne for the journeys it tried.
In the end, we will see, it's the laughter that we need,
As we chase down our pins, plant a smile, and succeed!

Seeking the Glimmer of Truth

In a world filled with questions, like socks lost at sea,
The truth shines like glitter, but where can it be?
We sift through the nonsense, the giggles and strife,
Trying to find the meaning of life!

With binoculars on, we scan through the crowd,
For wisdom hidden beneath laughter so loud.
Where wanders the truth? On a shoestring or kite?
In the midst of the chaos, we search for the light.

As we stumble and fumble, but never lose sight,
The truth's like a party that lasts through the night.
A riddle wrapped in a joke, absurd and surreal,
In the laughter we find the heart of the real.

So let's toast to our journey, raise a glass with a cheer,
For the truth that we seek brings the world ever near.
With a wink and a smile, we find joy in the quest,
Seeking glimmers of truth is simply the best!

Seeking the Hidden Thread

In a room filled with boxes, I sift and I scour,
Hoping to find what is lost in the hour.
The cat sees the yarn and jumps in delight,
While I hunt for the piece that just might be right.

With a wiggle and a giggle, I check under the couch,
But all that I find is a dusty old pouch.
That thread that I seek is a real tiny brat,
Maybe it's hiding, or perhaps it's a cat!

The clock ticks along, mocking my quest,
I tripped on a shoe, oh what a jest!
With a sigh and a laugh, I restart my pursuit,
If only my brain had a clear, straight route!

Amidst coffee stains, snack crumbs, and fluff,
I wonder if finding it feels like enough.
So I dance like a fool, my own little jig,
For in this great search, I'm quite the big gig!

Chasing Shadows of Existence

In the corner of shadows, I think and I ponder,
Searching for meaning, my thoughts start to wander.
Is it hidden in laughter? Or found in a sigh?
Maybe it's just where old socks like to lie!

With a magnifying glass, I roam through the fridge,
Convinced my lost piece is wedged by the wedge.
A pickle jars notes, while mustard takes bets,
That the missing item's on a journey, no stress!

I chase after whispers, I tickle the night,
With each tiny riddle, I giggle with fright.
Are the shadows alive? Do they play on my game?
Or hide as I tumble, rolling just the same?

Perhaps it's the laughter I seek for my prize,
Or ice cream on rooftops under starry skies.
So here's to the chase, a delightful charade,
Where shadows and giggles together parade!

Where Pieces Fail to Fit

I grabbed all the colors, laid them out wide,
Each piece had a story and some barely tried.
In a wild little dance, they just won't align,
The cat thinks it's art, I think it's a sign!

A corner I found, or maybe just flat?
With a frown and a chuckle, I ponder the mat.
Why's this one square? And why's that one round?
This puzzle's a joker, yet fun to confound!

With coffee in hand and crumbs on my shirt,
I start to believe that this game might be dirt.
A piece masquerading, just under my nose,
Who knew this was chaos, not fun, but a prose?

Yet, laughter erupts as I trip on my shoe,
This wild little giggle has brightened my view.
So what if they don't fit or end up askew?
I'll keep on exploring—a riddle's anew!

The Puzzle of Our Feelings

In the box of emotions, I delve here and there,
Each piece like a whisper, floaty in the air.
Happiness giggles, while sadness just sighs,
This puzzle's a wacky, colorful surprise!

I try to put love next to friendship so bright,
But they clash at the edges, and sigh with all might.
Confusion jumps in, wearing socks that don't match,
While joy just bursts out, in a dance and a scratch!

The pieces keep flipping, twist and whirl,
One minute I'm happy, next I might twirl.
Anger shows up, wearing polka dots bold,
With laughter in tow, this story unfolds!

Every emotion a puzzle, of colors and flair,
I'm learning to laugh, and just let down my hair.
So if I can't find that elusive last piece,
I'll go on a quest, and just dance in the breeze!